# WHAT WONDROUS HOPE

*A Service of Promise, Grace and Life*

*By Joseph M. Martin and Heather Sorenson*

*Orchestration by Ed Hogan*

(Tr. 1) This symbol indicates a track number on the ChoirTrax CD.

*Duration: ca. 50 Minutes*

ISBN 9-781-5400-6477-6

T0057858

Visit Hal Leonard Online at
**www.halleonard.com**

Visit Shawnee Press Online at
**www.shawneepress.com**

Contact Us:
**Hal Leonard**
7777 West Bluemound Road
Milwaukee, WI 53213
Email: info@halleonard.com

In Europe, contact:
**Hal Leonard Europe Limited**
Distribution Centre, Newmarket Road
Bury St Edmunds, Suffolk, IP33 3YB
Email: info@halleonardeurope.com

In Australia, contact:
**Hal Leonard Australia Pty. Ltd.**
4 Lentara Court
Cheltenham, Victoria, 3192 Australia
Email: info@halleonard.com.au

## FOREWORD

As we enter the final dark days of the Savior's life, we remember that there is hope in the face of despair. Knowing that His betrayal and crucifixion lay ahead, Jesus tried to prepare His disciples, assuring them that death would not be the end. But while He was with them, they could not imagine the desperate need for hope in the hours to come. In the words of Paul, "Hope that is seen is no hope at all. Who hopes for what they already have?" The challenge came for them, as it does for us, when the world seemed to close in around them, when the darkness of the tomb appeared to seal their own fate. Even in these somber days of Holy Week and the Passion, a ray of hope shines, for Easter is on the other side of the cross.

That wondrous hope is this: Love will triumph! A tree of death is not the end. Hope fulfilled is a tree of life! (Proverbs 13:12)

## PERFORMANCE NOTES

This work includes spoken parts for a pastor/worship leader and one narrator, but feel free to use as many narrators as you wish.

Two separate endings are included, depending on when the piece is performed. For Good Friday performances, the work ends at the crucifixion and closes with the anthem "What Wondrous Love Is This?," followed by an optional benediction. For those who perform the work on Easter, it ends at the resurrection and closes with the anthem "Easter Song." This ending also includes an optional benediction. Most of the anthems and their individual narrations can also function as standalone pieces for use during specific days of the season (from Palm Sunday through Easter).

For an added visual component, symbols (lamb, palm branches, cup, bread, pieces of silver, whip, crown of thorns, nails and cross) may be placed in the worship space or represented with banners. If you are using the work as a Tenebrae service, you may continue the tradition of draping the sanctuary symbols in black and/or removing the lighted Christ candle from the auditorium before the congregation exits in silence.

As always, we encourage you to adapt this template to meet your congregation's unique needs and to fit the worship style of your church.

# WHAT WONDROUS HOPE

## *Prologue:* UNTITLED

For Piano with Optional Instrumental Accompaniment

Duration: ca. 2:50

Music by
**HEATHER SORENSON**

WHAT WONDROUS HOPE – SATB

4

# THE GOSPEL OF HOPE

**Pastor:**

Loving God, we come together to remember your Son and His sacrifice for us.

Today we remember His life, which offered hope for every human need.
We give thanks that, through Him, there is:
rest for the weary and strength for the weak,
love for the lonely and acceptance for the rejected,
healing for the broken and comfort for the grieving.

We remember His death, which offers hope for our spiritual need.
We give thanks that, through Him, we have:
mercy and forgiveness of sin,
assurance in doubt,
and life after death.

Thank you for the gift that is ours through Jesus, the wondrous hope of the world.

Amen.

**Choir:**
*"Speak, O Lord"*

# Speak, O Lord

For SATB and Piano with Optional Instrumental Accompaniment

Duration: ca. 4:15

**Arranged by
JOSEPH M. MARTIN**

**Words and Music by
STUART TOWNEND
and KEITH GETTY**

10

WHAT WONDROUS HOPE – SATB

**Tr. 3**

glo - ry.

Teach us, Lord, full o - be - di - ence, Ho - ly rev - er - ence, true hu -

mil - i - ty.    *unis.*    Test    our    thoughts    and    our
*unis.*

at - ti - tudes in the ra - di - ance of Your

pur - i - ty. Cause our faith to rise, cause our

eyes to see Your ma - jes - tic love and au -

faith we'll walk as You walk with us.

Speak, O Lord, 'til Your church is built and the

earth is filled with Your glo - -

Tr. 5

**71 A little slower (♩ = ca. 68)**

Speak, O Lord, as we come to You to re-

ceive the food of Your Ho - ly Word.

# THE INVITATION TO HOPE

**Narrator:**

One day as John the Baptist was with two of his disciples, Jesus walked by. "Look," John said, "the Lamb of God." When they asked where He was going, Jesus said, "Come, and you will see," so they followed. One by one, He found them. "Come with me," He said, and they left their work and followed Him.

Wherever He went, Jesus invited them: the weary, the burdened, the sick, even little children. "If you are seeking, you will find what you're looking for in me. "Come to me," He called, "and I will not turn you away." He is still calling today.

**Choir:**
*"Come, Ye Seekers"*

# COME, YE SEEKERS

For SATB and Piano with Optional Instrumental Accompaniment

Duration: ca. 3:20

**Words by**
**JOSEPH M. MARTIN**
**and HEATHER SORENSON**

**Tune: RESTORATION**
**Additional Music and Arrangement by**
**HEATHER SORENSON**

WHAT WONDROUS HOPE – SATB

*Close to "m" quickly

WHAT WONDROUS HOPE – SATB

**Tr. 9**

**Tr. 11**

28

oh, there are ten thou - sand charms.

oh.

Ten thou - sand charms. Ten thou - sand

# THE ARMS OF HOPE

**Narrator:**

Throughout His ministry, Christ reached out to the forgotten and the unwanted, embracing the poor, the grieving, and the hopeless. He said, "I will never abandon you or leave you lonely. Very soon, I am going to prepare a place for you and when it is ready, I will come back for you and take you there to be with me."

A father to the fatherless and a defender of widows, God places the lonely in families. He makes a home for the homeless and leads the prisoner from darkness into freedom's light. He hears the cries of the lost and is close to the brokenhearted. In His arms, there is hope for us all.

**Choir:**
*"Home (The Arms of God)"*

# Home
## *The Arms of God*

For SATB and Piano with Optional Instrumental Accompaniment
Duration: ca. 4:15

**Words and Music by**
**HEATHER SORENSON**

soul that is dis-tressed,___ there is Rest.___ Ev-'ry

**17** Solo

prayer that has no voice___ or the free-dom to re-joice,___ from the

Soprano *mp*
Alto Oo,___
Tenor *mp*
oh.___
Bass

**17**

**Tr. 15**

dark-ness be re-leased:___ there is Peace.___ There is

36

home, _____ wel - come home. _____

O child, wel - come _____

And the arms ___ of God ___ will lead you all the ___ way.

home. And the arms ___ of God ___ will lead you all the ___ way.

*unis.*

Tr. 18

**Tr. 19**

**93**

*unis.* **mf**
Ev - 'ry sol - dier tired from war_____

*unis.* **mf**
who's been

**mf**

**mf**
rise on strength that's not your own,_____

shak - en to the core,_____

44

46

# THE JOY OF HOPE

**Narrator:**

As the Passover neared, Jesus made His way to Jerusalem. Word had spread that He had brought a dead man back to life, so when the people learned of His arrival they quickly lined the streets to see Him. Some of them hoped, while others already believed, that He was indeed the Messiah. They welcomed Him like royalty, spreading their coats on the ground and waving palm branches in the air. Running along beside Him, they shouted, "Blessed is He who comes in the name of the Lord! Hosanna to our King!"

But the religious leaders were upset and grumbled, "Look! He has mesmerized them all!" and they began plotting how they might get rid of Him.

**Choir:**
*"Hosanna"*

# HOSANNA
## *with "All Glory, Laud and Honor"*

For SATB, Children's Choir and Piano with Optional Instrumental Accompaniment

Duration: ca. 3:25

**Arranged by**
**JOSEPH M. MARTIN**

**Words and Music by**
**MICHAEL W. SMITH and**
**DEBORAH D. SMITH**

**Tr. 21** **With jubilant confidence** (♩ = ca. 124)

*Continue accents as in m. 8-9 throughout.

**ALL GLORY, LAUD AND HONOR**
Words by THEODULPH OF ORLEANS
Translated by JOHN MASON NEALE
Tune: ST. THEODULPH, Melchior Teschner

52

**Tr. 24**

Soprano / Alto

Ho - san - na, ho - san - na, ho - san - na!

Tenor / Bass

*div.*

Bless - ed is He who comes _____ in the name of the

Lord! Ho - san - na, ho - san - na, ho - san - na!

*sub. f*  *div.*

# THE PROMISE OF HOPE

**Narrator:**
Later in the week, Jesus and the disciples gathered for the Passover feast. While they were eating He told them, "One of you will betray me tonight." In disbelief, they asked themselves, "Am I the one?" Jesus took a loaf of bread and broke it, saying, "Take this bread and eat it. It is my body which will be broken for you." Then He took a cup of wine and said, "This is my blood which will be poured out to forgive the sins of many. Drink it and remember me. The next time I share it with you, it will be at my table in the kingdom of heaven."

**Choir:**
*"Behold the Lamb (Communion Hymn)"*

# Behold the Lamb
## *Communion Hymn*
For SATB and Piano with Optional Instrumental Accompaniment
Duration: ca. 4:35

**Arranged by**
**DOUGLAS NOLAN**

**Words and Music by**
**KEITH GETTY, STUART TOWNEND**
**and KRISTYN LENNOX GETTY**

© 2007 THANKYOU MUSIC (PRS)
This arrangement © 2013 THANKYOU MUSIC (PRS)
Admin. Worldwide at CAPITOLCMGPUBLISHING.COM excluding Europe
which is Admin. by INTEGRITY MUSIC, part of the David C. Cook family. SONGS@INTEGRITYMUSIC.COM
All Rights Reserved   Used by Permission

Bread of Life, and we drink_____ of His

sac - ri - fice, as a sign_____ of our bonds of peace_____

**Tr. 27**

a - round the ta - ble of the King.

**25** opt. Solos
*mp*

2. The bod - y of our Sav - ior, Je - sus Christ, torn for you;
3. The blood that cleans-es ev - 'ry stain of sin, shed for you,

eat and re - mem - ber the wounds that heal, the death that
drink and re - mem - ber He drained death's cup that all may

*2nd time to p. 65*  *All mf*

brings us life; paid the price to make us one. So we
en - ter in to re - ceive the life of

*2nd time to p. 65*

share ___ in this Bread of ___ Life, and we drink ___ of His

*unis.* *mf*
So we share in this Bread of ___ Life, ___ and we drink of His

*mf*

33

sac - ri - fice, as a sign _____ of our bonds of ___ love _____

36

*unis.*
a - round the ta - ble of the King.

*unis.*

39

WHAT WONDROUS HOPE – SATB

**Tr. 29**

**55** **A little slower (♩ = ca. 70)**

(+ Opt. Cong.)

And so with thank-ful-ness and faith we rise to re-

spond, and to re-mem-ber our call to fol-low in the

steps of Christ as His bod - y here on earth._____ As we

share_____ in His suf - fer - ing, we pro -

claim:_____ "Christ will come__ a - gain!" And we'll join_____ in the

68

WHAT WONDROUS HOPE – SATB

# THE CUP OF HOPE

**Narrator:**

After the meal, they went to a place called Gethsemane where Jesus asked them to keep watch. Kneeling in the darkness, He prayed, "Father, if there is any other way, please choose it. Yet even though I ask, I will do whatever you decide." When He returned, the disciples were asleep. "Can't you wait with me for one hour?" He asked them. Then He prayed a second time, "If it is possible, take this bitter cup away, but I will drink it if I must." Jesus returned again and told the disciples, "The time has come. Get up. My betrayer is here." No sooner had the words left His mouth than Judas arrived with the soldiers. As they arrested Him, the disciples scattered in fear for their own lives.

**Choir:**
*"Gethsemane Hymn"*

# Gethsemane Hymn

For SATB and Piano with Optional Instrumental Accompaniment

Duration: ca. 4:35

Arranged by
HEATHER SORENSON

Words and Music by
KEITH GETTY
and STUART TOWNEND

opt. Narration:
"Surely, He has borne our griefs and carried our sorrows. Yet we did esteem Him stricken, smitten of God,

and afflicted. But He was wounded for our transgressions, He was bruised for our iniquities: the chastisement of our peace was upon Him; and with His stripes, we are healed."

To see the King of __ Heav-en fall in

WHAT WONDROUS HOPE – SATB

72

74

satisfied and ev'ry sin is paid. _____ And satisfied. _____ ev'ry sin is paid. _____

**Optional epilogue**
**Slower, expressive (♩ = ca. 76)**

| 87 |

Sure - ly He has borne our griefs, car - ried all our

guilt and shame; bruised for our in - iq - ui - ties.

By His stripes we all are healed.

# WOUNDED HOPE

**Narrator:**

That night the religious leaders questioned Him, but Jesus refused to answer the charges against Him. Frustrated, the high priest finally asked, "Are you the Messiah, the Son of God?" Jesus replied, "I am who you say." At this, they found Him guilty of blasphemy, which carried the death penalty. Some of them spit on Him and beat Him with their fists. Others slapped Him in the face and mocked Him, "You are a prophet. Prophesy. Who hit you?"

*Good Friday performances should also include the following narration and may end with the optional benediction at the bottom of page 91.*

**Narrator:**

It was traditional to release one prisoner during the Passover, so the next morning, Pilate brought Jesus and a criminal named Barabbas to the people. "Who should I release, your king or Barabbas?" he asked. "Barabbas!" they shouted. "And what should I do with Jesus?" Pilate asked them. "Crucify Him!" they answered. So the guards took Jesus away. After they beat Him, they put a purple robe across His back and shoved a crown of thorns on His head, laughing at Him. Then they nailed His hands and feet to a cross and crucified Him. Looking at the crowd, Jesus said, "Father, forgive them. They don't know what they are doing." And the Lamb of God cried out and died for them--and for us.

**Choir:**
*"What Wondrous Love Is This?"*

# What Wondrous Love Is This?

For SATB, Congregation and Piano with Optional Instrumental Accompaniment

Duration: ca. 4:45

**Arranged by
HEATHER SORENSON**

**Traditional Folk Hymn
Additional Words and Music by
HEATHER SORENSON**

Lyrics: What won-drous love is this, O my soul, O my

WHAT WONDROUS HOPE – SATB

*Original text: "peace"

WHAT WONDROUS HOPE – SATB

84

on, I'll sing on. And through e - ter - ni -

*unis.* **mf**

**mf**

**mf**

(– Cong.)

95

ty, I'll sing on.

**mp**

Tr. 37

*rit.*

*rit.*

*rit.*

WHAT WONDROUS HOPE – SATB

# THE LAMB OF HOPE

**Narrator:**

It was traditional to release one prisoner during the Passover, so the next morning, Pilate brought Jesus and a criminal named Barabbas to the people. "Who should I release, your king or Barabbas?" he asked. "Barabbas!" they shouted. "And what should I do with Jesus?" Pilate asked them. "Crucify Him!" they answered. So the guards took Jesus away. After they beat Him, they put a purple robe across His back and shoved a crown of thorns on His head, laughing at Him. Then they nailed His hands and feet to a cross and crucified Him. Looking at the crowd, Jesus said, "Father, forgive them. They don't know what they are doing." And the Lamb of God cried out and died for them--and for us.

**Choir:**
*"Mercy Tree"*

*Good Friday performances should omit the above narration*
*and may end with the following benediction.*
*"Mercy Tree" should not be sung. The congregation exits in silence,*
*or the Prologue "Untitled" can be repeated as a postlude or epilogue.*

*Easter performances end with a different benediction after "Easter Song."*

**Pastor:**

There is no greater love than this: to give one's life for his friends.

Even on the cross, the arms of love are open wide. In their silence, they are saying: "Come to me, all of you, and find what you seek. I will not turn you away."

In His arms there is room, and hope, for all.

# Mercy Tree

### For SATB and Piano with Optional Instrumental Accompaniment

Duration: ca. 5:20

Arranged by
JOSEPH M. MARTIN

Words and Music by
MICHAEL WILLIAM NEALE
and KRISSY NORDHOFF

soul,_____ find your _ rest and be made____ whole._____

**19**

____ Stripes of blood that stain its frame_____ shed to

wash a - way our shame. From the scars, pure love re -

**Tr. 39**                    *end Solo*

leased: sal - va - tion by the mer - cy____ tree.____

"It is fin - ished," was His cry.____ The per - fect Lamb was cru - ci - fied. His sac - ri - fice, our vic to - ry; our Sav - ior chose the mer - cy tree.

96

WHAT WONDROUS HOPE – SATB

come; He has ris-en from the _____ dead.

Tr. 42

*unis.* **mp**

One day soon we'll see His

*unis.* **mp**

# LIVING HOPE

**Narrator:**

Because of the Sabbath, there was no time to prepare the body of Jesus for burial. So early in the morning on the first day of the week, the women went to the tomb. When they got there, the large stone blocking its entrance had been rolled away. An angel sat upon it and he said, "Why do you look for the living in a place for the dead? He is not here. He has risen, just as He said. Hurry and tell the disciples. He is alive!" When they realized what the angel had said, they were overcome with joy. They ran as fast as they could to share the news, the words ringing in their ears: "He is alive! He is alive! He is alive!"

**Choir:**
*"Easter Song"*

# EASTER SONG

*with "Easter Song Hear the Bells Ringing" and "Christ the Lord Is Risen Today"*

For SATB and Piano with Optional Instrumental Accompaniment

Duration: ca. 3:35

Arranged by
**JOSEPH M. MARTIN**

Words and Music by
**ANNE HERRING**

**CHRIST THE LORD IS RISEN TODAY**
Words by CHARLES WESLEY, Music Adapted from LYRA DAVIDICA
Copyright © 2017 by HAL LEONARD – MILWIN MUSIC CORP.
International Copyright Secured  All Rights Reserved

**EASTER SONG HEAR THE BELLS RINGING**
© 1974 LATTER RAIN MUSIC (ASCAP)
Copyright Renewed
This arrangement © 2017 LATTER RAIN MUSIC (ASCAP)
Admin. at CAPITOLCMGPUBLISHING.COM
All Rights Reserved  Used by Permission

WHAT WONDROUS HOPE – SATB

unis.
now, go tell His dis - ci - ples that Je - sus
48
Christ is no long - er dead!"
Christ is no long - er, no long - er dead!"
52
Tr. 47
58
f
Joy to the world,
f
f
56

110

heav'n's, and earth re - ply, Al - le - lu - ia!

poco a poco cresc.

mf

114

116

Tr. 50

WHAT WONDROUS HOPE – SATB

WHAT WONDROUS HOPE – SATB

# THE ASSURANCE OF HOPE

**Pastor:**

Go now with love. This is love: Not that we loved God first, but that He loved us. And we know His love because He sent us His one and only Son.

Go with grace, which is the undeserved gift of mercy, freely offered by God. We received His grace when Christ gave His life in place of our own, that we might be saved.

Go with hope, which is the confident waiting for what God has promised. We received hope with the promise that the power which raised Christ from the dead, will one day raise us to eternal life with Him.

Finally, go with God's assurance: "Those who hope in me will not be disappointed." He is faithful to keep His promise. What wondrous love, what wondrous grace, what wondrous hope is ours through Him! Thanks be to God!